Dear Parents/Teachers:

Yay! Your child/student is interest in
The goal: reading on their own and lc

Waldorf Readers are designed to help your child/student enjoy the learning process. Our Readers have 4 levels to guide your child/student to independent reading.

Each level collection has interesting stories, unique characters and colorful illustrations. All Waldorf Readers are original works with characters your child/student will enjoy. Waldorf Publishing strives to accommodate a full reading experience for any child/student at any reading level.

Waldorf Readers will entertain your child/student level by level.

Spark Reading   **Preschool-Kindergarten**
-Large font and easy words
-Illustrations to accompany the storyline
-No more than two syllables

Level 1 Waldorf Readers introduce children/students to reading. Sentences are short and simple. Using phonics skills, children/students will sound out words.

Read Together   **Preschool-Grade 1**
-Short sentences
-Easy to understand stories
-Simple vocabulary
-No more than two syllables

Level 2 Waldorf Readers keep the excitement for reading strong. Sentences will include bigger words and more in depth story lines, which are sure to entertain.

Independent Reading   **Grade 1-3**
-Exciting and relatable characters
-Plots and story lines that are relatable and easy to follow
-Topics children enjoy
-No more than 3 syllable words

Level 3 Waldorf Readers have larger paragraphs and words that will challenge and engage children/students.

Advanced Independent Reading   **Grade 2-4**
-In depth plot and story lines
-Larger blocks of text
-Full color illustration
-Words with 3+ syllables

Level 4 Waldorf Readers are more challenging and lengthy. These books are perfect for children/students who want to read longer books and still enjoy colorful illustrations. Level 4 Waldorf Readers are the last level before advancing to Waldorf Chapter Books.

Published by Waldorf Publishing
2140 Hall Johnson Road
#102-345
Grapevine, Texas 76051
www.WaldorfPublishing.com

Anne Sullivan: Courageous Kids

ISBN: 978-1-64764-850-3

Library of Congress Control Number: 2020937041

Illustrations by Carson Arnold-Anderson
Design by Baris Celik

Courageous Kids:
Anne Sullivan
Finds a Home

WALDORF PUBLISHING

Map of
NEW ENGLAND

Maine

Vermont

New
Hampshire

Massachusetts

Feeding Hill

Boston

Connecticut

Rhode Island

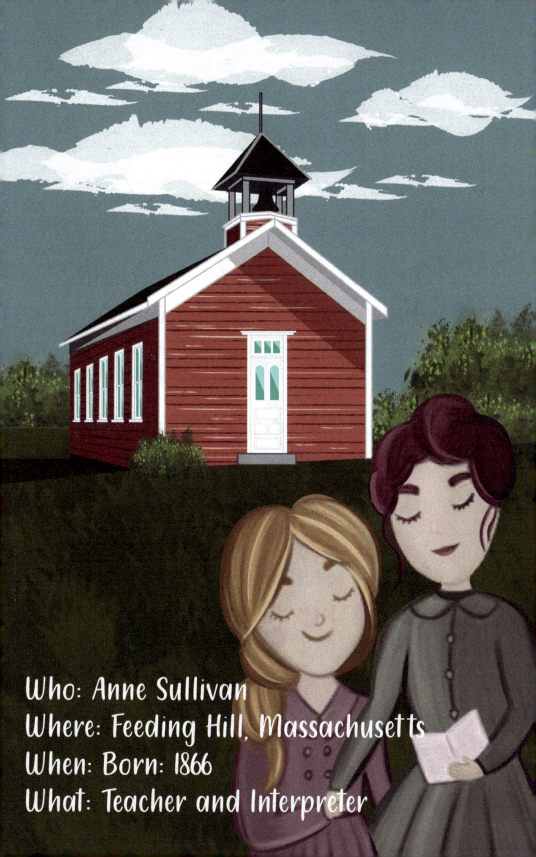

Who: Anne Sullivan
Where: Feeding Hill, Massachusetts
When: Born: 1866
What: Teacher and Interpreter

The nurse studied ten-year-old Anne and her seven-year-old brother, Jimmie.

The nurse kept asking questions and scribbling on her piece of paper.

Anne frowned and answered her questions.

"Our father can't afford us,"
Anne said, "That's why he
sent us to the poorhouse.

Our mother died two years
ago. Jimmie has a disease
in his hip. It's hard for him
to walk."

The nurse glanced at Jimmie.
Jimmie hid behind Anne.

"Don't worry," Anne whispered.
"I'll take care of you."

Annie kept answering the nurse's questions.

"I had a bad infection in my eyes when I was five," Anne continued. "I can't see very well."

Finally, the nurse laid her pencil down. "Jimmie will go to the men's section," she said. "Anne, you will go to the women's section."

Anne grabbed Jimmie. She stared at the nurse.

"My brother stays with me," she yelled. "He's not well! He needs me."

"We have rules," the nurse said. "Jimmie must go to the men's section."

Anne began screaming and yelling. "He stays with me!"

Finally, the nurse shrugged her shoulders. "Alright," the nurse said. "Your brother can stay with you. But you have to stay with the sick people."

Anne and Jimmie hurried behind the nurse as she strode down the long, dingy hallways. They kept looking at the people in the crowded, dirty rooms.

Some people were sick. Some people were crying. Some people stared at nothing. Anne whispered to Jimmie, "At least we are together," she said.

Three months later, the sickness took Jimmie. A lady in their room kept saying, "Don't cry. He went to heaven." But Anne cried anyway.

After that, Anne decided to find a way to leave that crowded, dingy place.

Some people called inspectors came to the poorhouse. The inspectors looked in the rooms and asked questions. They wanted to know if the people were safe.

Anne waited until the inspector was ready to go. Then she grabbled the inspector's jacket, "Please, get me out of here!" she pleaded. "I want to go to school."

The inspector helped Anne.

The inspector sent Anne to a school for blind children. Anne was so excited to leave and get a new start!

But when Anne got to the new school, the other students did not like her. Anne did not have a nightgown or a hairbrush or any nice clothes.

Anne could not read. She had bad manners. The other students made fun of her.

But Anne stayed strong. She learned to read braille. She learned to use sign language. She made friends.

At the school, a doctor operated on Anne's eyes. She could see much better! She graduated at the top of her class!

After she finished school, Anne took a job teaching a seven-year-old girl named Helen Keller. Helen was blind and deaf.

When Helen was a toddler, she got sick with a terrible fever. When the fever was gone, Helen could not see or hear.Her parents did now know how to help her.

When Anne arrived, she was shocked when we saw Helen Keller. Helen did not have any manners.

When the family sat down to eat, Helen walked around the table. Helen kept sticking her hands onto everyone's plate and grabbing any food she wanted.

Helen made a mess.

Anne pushed Helen's hand away. She did not allow Helen to take food from her plate. Helen threw a fit. She stomped and cried.

But Anne made Helen learn manners. In a short time, Anne taught Helen how to sit and eat at the table! Then she began teaching Helen to read.

WHAT
HAPPENED?

Anne was a wonderful teacher. She used sign language to spell words into Helen's hands.

One time, while Helen's hands were under water, Anne kept spelling "water" into Helen's hand. Suddenly, Helen understood!

Helen raced around the yard touching trees and grass and holding out her hand. Anne laughed with happiness and signed the names onto Helen's hand.

In a short time, Helen
learned over 600 words.
Helen learned to read and
write!

Anne became famous for
teaching Helen how to
understand.

CPSIA information can be obtained
at www.ICGtesting.com
Printed in the USA
LVHW011329210121
676966LV00005B/279